THE Crocodilians

REMINDERS OF THE AGE OF DINOSAURS

• PHYLLIS J. PERRY •

A First Book

Franklin Watts

A Division of Grolier Publishing

New York ◆ London ◆ Hong Kong ◆ Sydney

Danbury, Connecticut

To Julia, Clare, and Casey

---

*With thanks to Jim Van Abbema of the
American Museum of Natural History for his
helpful comments on the manuscript.*

Cover and Interior Design by Molly Heron
Maps created by Vantage Art
Photographs ©: American Museum of Natural History: 8, 10;
Corbis-Bettmann: 51 bottom; Dembinsky Photo Assoc.: 23, 25, 28 (Stan Osolinski);
Photo Researchers: 6 (Eric & Dave Hosking), 27 (J. H. Robinson), 43
(Jany Sauvanet), 38 (Lawrence Naylor), 52, 55 (Nigel J. Dennis), 32 (Rod Planck),
Cover, 46 (Tom McHugh); Superstock, Inc.: 16; UPI/Corbis-Bettmann: 36;
Visuals Unlimited: 51 top (A&E Morris), 33 (Joe McDonald), 44 (Ken Lucas), 21
(Kirtley-Perkins), 14 (Max & Bea Hunn), 4 (Milton H. Tierney, Jr.).

Library of Congress Cataloging-in-Publication Data

Perry, Phyllis Jean.
Crocodilians: reminders of the days of dinosaurs / Phyllis J. Perry
p. cm. (A First book)
Includes bibliographical references and index.
Summary: Describes the physical characteristics, habitats, and life cycles
of the group of reptiles known as the crocodilians, which includes
alligators, crocodiles, caimans, and gavials.
ISBN 0-531-20254-2 (lib. bdg.)   ISBN 0-531-15856-X (pbk.)
1. Crocodilia—Juvenile literature.   [1. Crocodilia. 2. Alligators 3. Crocodiles]
I. Title.   II. Series.
    QL666.C9p47   1997
    597.98—dc20   96-25875 CIP AC

Contents

CHAPTER 1
Dinosaurs and Crocodilians

A strange-looking beast swims quietly through the murky swamp water. Its gray skin, partly covered in green pond scum, blends perfectly with its surroundings. The creature holds its broad, round snout just above the water's surface. Its massive, 12-foot (3.7-m) body is covered with small, hard spikes that are visible from shore. Watching this alligator, it takes very little imagination to picture another scene that took place more than a million years ago.

Teleosaurus, a prehistoric sea crocodile, swims to shore. As the teleosaur crawls onto land, it has no idea that a gigantic Megalosaurus is lurking behind shoreline vegetation. The megalosaur waits patiently until the crocodile is very close. Suddenly, the megalosaur lunges forward and grabs the crocodile in its huge jaws. The startled crocodile struggles

fiercely against its attacker. A terrible, bloody fight begins.

None of us will ever see one of these fierce battles because dinosaurs, including Megalosaurus, began to die out about 65 million years ago. For millions and millions of years before that, however, crocodiles and dinosaurs shared the Earth. You might even consider them to be cousins. They belong to a group of *reptiles* called the *archosaurs*.

While dinosaurs are long gone, crocodiles and alligators are still among us today. Both crocodiles and alligators belong to a group of reptiles called the *crocodilians*. There are twenty-two species of crocodilians living on Earth today.

A great deal of what scientists know about dinosaurs is based on what they have learned by studying crocodilians. They are reminders of the Age of Dinosaurs.

The long body of this alligator looks like a log as it floats in the green pond scum.

TIME SCALE OF EARTH HISTORY

Time Scale	ERAS	Duration of Periods	PERIODS			DOMINANT ANIMAL LIFE
	CENOZOIC 70 MILLION YEARS DURATION		Quaternary		Recent Pleistocene	Man
10 20 40 60		70	Tertiary	EPOCHS	Pliocene Miocene Oligocene Eocene Paleocene	Mammals
80 100	**MESOZOIC** 120 MILLION YEARS DURATION	50	Cretaceous			
150		35	Jurassic			
		35	Triassic			Dinosaurs
200	**PALEOZOIC** 350 MILLION YEARS DURATION	25	Permian			
		20	Pennsylvanian			
250		30	Mississippian			Primitive reptiles
300		65	Devonian			Amphibians
350		35	Silurian			Fishes
400		75	Ordovician			
450		90	Cambrian			Invertebrates
500	FPO #2					
PROTEROZOIC ARCHAEOZOIC *Figures in millions of years*		*Figures in millions of years*	1500 million years duration			Beginnings of life

Time Scale — Figures in millions of years

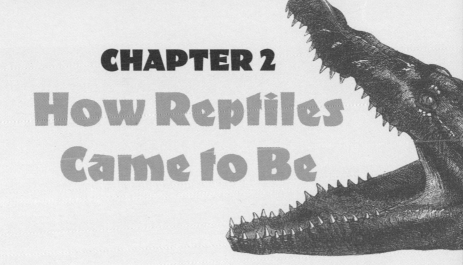

CHAPTER 2
How Reptiles Came to Be

At one time, there was no life on Earth. The first living things developed in the oceans. They had just one cell and resembled algae. Over millions and millions of years, more and more complex organisms *evolved*. By studying *fossils*, scientists have learned that at the very beginning of Devonian times (340 million years ago), descendants of some fishes came out onto the land. These creatures were the earliest *amphibians*.

Although amphibians live most of their adult lives on land, they must lay their eggs in the water. From these eggs, tadpoles hatch. The tadpoles live in the water until they grow legs and lose their gills. Then, they too move onto the land.

Over time, reptiles—including the earliest members of the crocodilian family tree—developed from some of these amphibians. Reptiles have been on

Fossil remains help scientists determine how ancient beasts such as Deinosuchus might have looked.

Earth for approximately 300 million years. During the Age of Reptiles, dinosaurs were the most spectacular creatures. But there were other reptiles as well as amphibians and mammals living at the same time.

Unlike amphibians, reptiles do not lay eggs in the

water. Both the ancient dinosaurs and crocodilians laid their eggs on land. These eggs had tough shells that retained moisture. When an egg hatched, a miniature version of the adult came out and began its life among the huge tree ferns, mosses, and primitive trees.

The Age of Reptiles spanned three periods of geologic history: the Triassic, Jurassic, and Cretaceous periods. These periods stretch nearly 120 million years. Scientists believe that the very first crocodilians appeared on Earth during the Triassic period.

The earliest ancestors of the crocodilians, the *protosuchians*, lived about 200 million years ago. Their bodies, which were covered with bony plates, were about 3 feet (1 m) long. The protosuchians also had very sharp teeth. They lived in North America, South America, Africa, and the eastern part of Asia.

About 180 million years ago, Stenosaurus, a crocodile-like reptile, lived on the sandy shores of prehistoric oceans in Europe, northern Africa, North America, and South America. Like the crocodiles of today, stenosaurs probably sunned themselves on the beach during the day. These reptiles were between 12 and 20 feet (3.7 and 6.1 m) long.

Fossils found in the United States show that one ancient relative of the modern crocodile, Deinosuchus, sometimes grew to be 50 feet (15 m) in length. This

world. Alligators live in the southern United States, the West Indies, Central America, the northern part of South America, and in the Yangtze River area of China. Caimans are found in southern Mexico, Central America, and the northern part of South America. Gavials live in India, Pakistan, and Bangladesh. Crocodiles are found in North America, South America, Australia, Africa, and Asia.

Although crocodilians are divided into three separate groups and live in many different parts of the world, the lifestyles of all crocodilians are very similar. The next chapter will provide you with an in-depth look at the physical characteristics and behavior of alligators. This information will also help you to better understand caimans as well as gavials and crocodiles.

Alligators spend much of their lives in water, but they have lungs and are able to breathe and walk on land.

The American alligator is a common sight in the Everglades National Park in Florida.

CHAPTER 4
Alligators

There are two species of alligators: the Chinese alligator and the American alligator.

The Chinese alligator, which lives in the lower Yangtze River valley of China, is blackish-olive with faint yellow bands. It has a very broad, bluntly-rounded snout and grows to a length of about 6 feet (1.9 m). There is a prominent bony plate beneath the eyelids of Chinese alligators.

The American alligator can be found in the southern part of the United States, the West Indies, Central America, and the northern part of South America. It is slightly larger than the Chinese alligator. The young have more yellow crossbands on their tails and bodies, and the bony plate under each eyelid is barely visible.

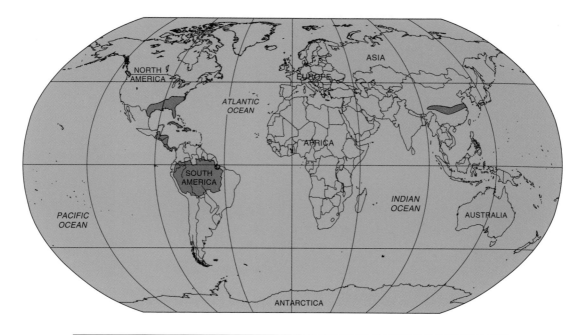

Alligators can be found in the areas shaded red.

When Spanish explorers first discovered an alligator in Florida, they called it "el lagarto," which means "the lizard." Over time, the pronunciation of el lagarto changed to alligator.

In the United States, the American alligator is found as far north as North Carolina and as far west as central Texas and the lower Rio Grande. The most well-known home of the American alligator is the Everglades National Park in Florida. The park consists of saltwater marshes and coastal swamps.

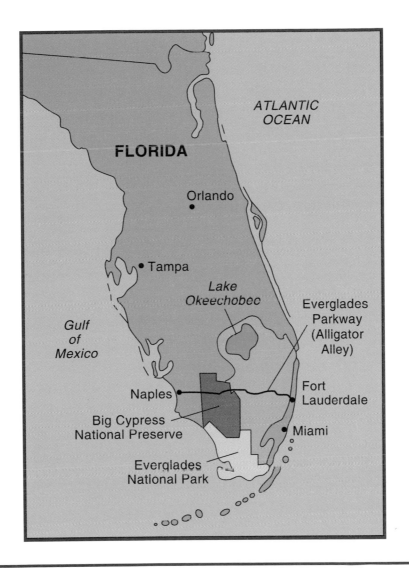

American alligators are so common in the Everglades region of Florida that the Everglades Parkway, which runs between Naples and Fort Lauderdale, is sometimes called Alligator Alley.

An Alligator's Life

Watching a female alligator preparing to lay her eggs reminds some people of the way a bird makes a nest. The female alligator builds her nest with great care because she is likely to use it year after year, making repairs each spring as they are needed.

First, the female alligator chooses a site close to the water's edge. She clears an area the size of a small bedroom, piles plants and grasses on top, and packs them down by crawling over them. Next, she hollows out a little area in the center of the mound and fills the hole with mud and water. Then she makes another hole in the center of her nest, straddles the nest with her hind legs, and begins laying eggs.

It will take about 30 minutes for her to lay her *clutch* of thirty-five to forty eggs. The eggs, which have white shells, look something like goose eggs. The mother alligator covers her eggs with wet leaves and mud, then presses and smoothes the nest with her body. The completed nest is about the size of a double bed. Making the nest and laying the eggs takes about 3 days.

A baby alligator grows inside its shell for about 9 weeks. During this time, its body is curled with its back to the shell and its tail tucked between its hind legs. A cord running between the baby and the egg's

It takes a female alligator about 3 days to make a nest and lay her clutch of eggs.

yolk provides the baby with the nutrients it needs to grow. Blood vessels in the membrane around the baby provide it with oxygen. This oxygen enters the egg through tiny holes in the shell.

For the baby to grow, the egg must stay warm and moist. Heat from the sun keeps the inside of the nest about 5°F (3°C) warmer than the surrounding air. Moisture comes from the rain that falls on the decaying material covering the nest.

Alligator eggs are exposed to many dangers. Raccoons, bears, opossums, and skunks often dig up and eat the eggs. Some mother alligators keep a watchful eye on their nests. If the alligator notices an intruder, she may charge after it. In most cases, she will first try to frighten the enemy away by inhaling air slowly and then expelling it quickly through her mouth. This action causes a hissing noise.

When baby alligators are ready to hatch, they make grunting noises. Sometimes the mother alligator hears the grunts and helps the young by clearing away the top of the mound. Each baby pushes through its shell with a special pointed spike, or *egg tooth*, at the tip of its upper jaw. As soon as it is free of its shell, the baby searches for the water.

Baby alligators are dark (almost black) with yellow stripes on their tails and sides. They weigh about 2 ounces (62 g) and are 8 to 9 inches (20 to 23 cm)

Baby alligators face many dangers when they first emerge from their shells. They stay close to their mother for protection from enemies.

long. They appear to run on their tiptoes and make high-pitched grunts. The grunt of a mother alligator calling her young sounds something like a pig's oink. During the first few days of life, the bellies of baby alligators are swollen because they are still receiving nutrition from the unabsorbed yolk sac. This swelling and the egg tooth gradually disappear.

Soon the baby alligators are ready to hunt for food. Using their needle-sharp teeth, baby alligators will catch and eat minnows, tadpoles, moths, water beetles, flies, and grasshoppers. As they grow larger, they will attack crayfish, small frogs, and toads.

Many alligator babies stay near their mother during their first year of life. The alligators live in a "gator hole," which the mother digs in the bottom of a river or lake. The mother widens the hole each year by tearing out water plants. By doing this, the alligators also make a better habitat for waterfowl, fishes, and muskrats. During summer dry spells, gator holes are sometimes the only remaining source of habitable water.

Baby alligators face many enemies: raccoons, bobcats, mink, otters, bullfrogs, great horned owls, American egrets, garfish, snapping turtles, cottonmouth snakes, and even adult alligators. As many as half of all young alligators may be eaten during their first weeks and months of life.

Young alligators are about 9 inches (23 cm) long and have yellow stripes on their tails and sides.

The alligators that survive double in size in 2 months. After this initial growth spurt, they continue to grow about 12 inches (30 cm) each year until they are about 6 years old. At this point, they are considered adults. Adult alligators continue to grow, but at a slower rate.

Alligators spend the winter (October to March) in dens that they have built in swamps or the banks of streams. These dens are normally submerged and must be accessed from underwater tunnels that can be 15 feet (4.6 m) long. A wide spot, which forms an underground pool with an air pocket around it, may be at the back of the tunnel. Trails, called *crawls*, can often be seen leading through swamp grasses to alligator dens.

When making its den, an alligator uses its snout like a shovel and kicks the loosened dirt away with its hind feet. Then, by waving its tail back and forth, the alligator is able to create a current that carries away excess silt, so that it will not block the entrance to the den.

One of the safest places for American alligator babies to rest is right on their mother's head.

This American alligator in the Florida Everglades is eating a garfish, one of its favorite meals.

Some mother alligators keep their small alligators in the den with them during the first winter. (Occasionally very old male alligators live in their dens year round, coming out only to eat.)

When it begins to get cold, alligators get sluggish and lose interest in eating. They do not truly *hibernate,* but they do become *torpid* in their dens. On especially warm winter days, alligators may come out to sun themselves. In the spring, alligators leave their dens. At this time, many yearling alligators leave their mothers' pools and set out on their own.

Mating takes place in the water from April to June. Male and female alligators both bellow and give off an odor from musk glands under their snouts. This odor may help them to find each other, so that mating can occur.

Alligators bellow at other times, too. The alligator roars by lifting its head out of the water and taking several deep breaths. It fills its lungs with air and then, by a series of body contractions, forces air out of its partly open mouth. This action causes flexible bits of skin located between body plates to vibrate, making ripples and bubbles in the water.

Alligators like to sun by day and eat by night. Adult alligators eat water snakes, muskrats, rabbits, turtles, birds, garfish, catfish, and snails. They are more apt to lie in wait for food than to go out in search of it.

Alligators have been known to attack humans, but this is rare. Their bad reputation probably comes from confusing them with crocodiles, which are much more aggressive. Very large male alligators may attack mammals such as dogs, pigs, and cattle. Alligators clamp their jaws around these animals and pull them under water until they drown.

The Alligator Body

Although there are fossil records of huge alligators, most of today's adult alligators are 6 to 12 feet (1.8 to 3.7 m) long. Females, which are seldom more than 9 feet (2.7 m) long, usually weigh about 160 pounds (73 kg).

Full-grown alligators blend well with their swamp environment. When they are wet, alligators look black, and when they are dry, their scales are a dull gray-green color. Their bellies are pale yellow.

Alligators have short, strong legs, which allow them to walk and run on land. They can run very quickly for short distances. Their hind legs are longer than their front legs. Their front feet have five toes, while their hind feet have only four. There are claws on the three inner toes of each webbed foot.

Alligators are very fast swimmers. To swim, they hold their legs close to their bodies and move their strong tails from side to side. When alligators float near the surface of the water, they may use their webbed hind feet to tread water.

An alligator's eyes are located on the top of its head. As a result, they stick up above the water's surface while the rest of the alligator is submerged. Each eye has a vertical pupil, which contracts to a vertical slit in bright light. At noon, the pupils are narrow slits, but after dark the pupils widen so that more light can enter.

This is similar to the way human eyes, with round pupils, contract in bright light and dilate in dim light. In the alligator eye, there is a reflective layer behind the retina that contains guanine crystals. This mirror-like layer reflects most of the incoming light back through the light-receptor cells of the eye, producing the red eye shine that is familiar to nighttime crocodilian observers.

An alligator's nostrils also stick up above the water. As a result, alligators can lay almost completely hidden under water while still being able to see and breathe.

An alligator can remain completely submerged for a long time. A transparent membrane slides back to cover its eyes, a muscular valve closes to keep water out of its nostrils, and flaps of skin shut to prevent water from entering its ear openings.

Because an alligator's eyes are on top of its head, and its nostrils stick up, an alligator can be almost completely hidden in the water while still being able to see and breathe.

An alligator's throat is also specially adapted to life in the water. The alligator has a broad tongue, which is attached to its lower jaw. The tongue can be raised

Alligators have sharp teeth. These teeth help the alligator to catch and tear apart its food.

to keep water out of its throat. Although the crocodilian tongue can be raised and lowered, it does not move forward and backward (as your tongue does).

Every alligator has a special fold of skin at the back of its mouth. When this flap is closed, the alligator's windpipe is separated from its mouth cavity. As a result, alligators can grasp and wrestle with *prey* without fear of drowning. Alligators feed heavily in the summer and store up fat for the winter.

Alligators have broad, rounded snouts that can close with tremendous force. Once closed, however, an alligator's jaws can be held shut by the hands of a strong man.

Alligators have sharp teeth that can break right through the bones of most animals. They use their teeth to catch and tear apart animals, not to chew food into small pieces. Crocodilian teeth are not venomous. In other words, they do not have special fangs that release a poison into their prey. (Snakes, another kind of reptile, do release a poison into their victims.)

An alligator's teeth are replaced a number of times during its life. When cleaning, zoo workers often find several teeth in the alligators' pools. When its mouth is closed, an alligator's upper teeth close outside its lower ones. An extra-long bottom fourth tooth on each side of the mouth fits into a pit in the alligator's upper jaw when its mouth is closed.

The alligator has a well-developed hard palate (the upper inside part of its mouth) to protect its brain against possible kicks from animals caught in its jaws. When an alligator catches a meal in its jaws, it rolls over and over in the water, thrashing and twisting until the animal is dead and torn apart. The alligator swallows large pieces as they twist off. An alligator does not chew its food, but special strong digestive juices in its stomach allow the alligator to eat an animal, fur, feathers, bones, and all!

Protecting Alligators

Alligators have no enemies, except man. Their sides, legs, and bellies are covered with rows of small horny scales, while the head and back are sheathed with scales made of hard rings of bone. This protective waterproof hide is almost as strong as metal.

Because alligator hides are valuable, hunters have killed so many of these animals that they are close to extinction. It is amazing that humans have nearly killed off a group of creatures that was able to survive when the dinosaurs could not. Between the years 1800 and 1900, approximately 3 million alligators were killed in Florida.

To save alligators from extinction, many states passed laws limiting or forbidding the killing of alligators. Since it was listed as an endangered species by the U.S. Fish and Wildlife Service in 1967, the

American alligator has made a remarkable comeback. In 1977, it was reclassified as a threatened species.

In 1947, a large portion of the Everglades region in Florida was set aside as a national park. Everglades National Park features wooden walkways above some of the swamp areas, allowing visitors to see alligators in their natural environment. The Everglades region includes more than 2,700 square miles (7,000 sq. km) of land between Lake Okeechobee and the Gulf of Mexico.

Because alligators living in their natural setting are protected from hunters, many alligators are now raised commercially on farms in Florida, Louisiana, Georgia, and South Carolina. The oldest and largest alligator farm in the United States is in St. Augustine, Florida. At times, this farm may have as many as 6,000 alligators.

In 1924, these alligator hunters shot this 12-foot (4 m) alligator fourteen times, and then killed it with a hatchet.

A spectacled caiman catches a fish.

CHAPTER 5
Caimans and Gavials

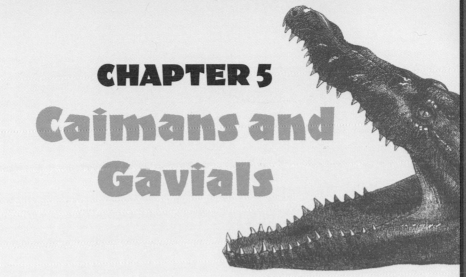

Caimans are more closely related to alligators than other crocodilians. Their teeth fit together like those of the alligators, but their snouts are much narrower. Like alligators, caimans build their nests with vegetation and lay between thirty and fifty eggs. Caimans are much noisier than alligators; they make a variety of growling, croaking, and snorting noises.

There are five species of caimans. The smallest caiman, Curvier's dwarf caiman, is found along the upper Amazon River of South America (in the Orinoco and São Francisco river basins) and in Paraguay's river systems. Adults are usually 4 to 5 feet (1.2 to 1.5 m) long. This caiman has a short snout and a doglike skull. It lives in flooded forests around major lakes and probably eats invertebrates and fish.

The spectacled caiman or common caiman is

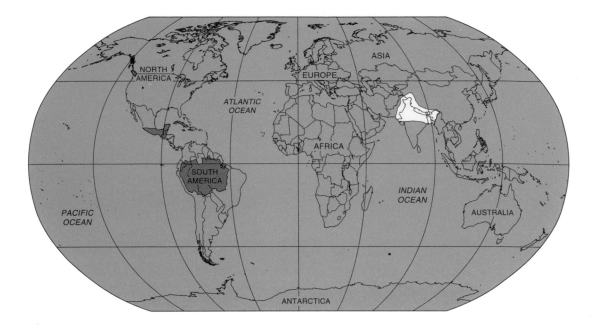

Caimans can be found in the areas shaded red, and gavials can be found in the area shaded yellow.

generally 7 to 8 feet (2.1 to 2.4 m) long. It is found in southern Mexico, Central America, and South America. This caiman gets its name from the curved, bony crosswise ridge that is right in front of its eyes. This ridge resembles a pair of glasses. The upper eyelids of this caiman look swollen and wrinkled. In some animals, the eyelids resemble little blunt horns.

Each female caiman builds a nest mound in which she lays fifteen to forty eggs. This caiman eats insects, crabs, water snails, and fish. At one time, spectacled caimans were sold in pet stores.

The Schneider's dwarf or smooth-fronted caiman, found in tropical South America, is the most abundant species of crocodilian. These caimans are 4.5 to 5.5 feet (1.4 to 1.7 m) in length. They have short, broad tails, and often spend time away from the water. They wander more than half a mile (800 m) from streams and hide among vegetation or in hollow logs.

These caimans make their nests at the end of the dry season. Each clutch contains ten to fifteen eggs. The eggs hatch at the beginning of the rainy season. The hatchlings eat insects, while juveniles feed on snakes, birds, and lizards. The adults include mammals such as porcupines and pacas in their diets.

The broad-snouted caiman, which also lives in tropical South America, grows from 6.5 to 10 feet (2 to 3 m) in length. It has a broad, bluntly rounded snout that resembles an alligator's. Its eyelids develop into horns like those of the spectacled caiman. The abdomen is a dull white color, its sides are light brown, and its back is dark or olive-brown with round, brown patches. These caimans have brown patches on their sides, snouts, and tails.

They live in freshwater swamps and in mangroves around the margins of lakes and rivers. The females lay thirty to sixty eggs. These caimans eat insects, crustaceans, water snails, fish, mammals, and birds.

The largest of the New World crocodilians is the black caiman, which may be 20 feet (6.1 m) long. This animal, which is found in the upper Amazon River area of South America, is a glossy, black color with a whitish or yellow abdomen.

The black caiman has flat, wrinkled eyelids and a snout that is bluntly rounded at the tip. Young black caimans have black bars adjacent to their eyes and yellow cross-stripes on their backs and tails. Black caimans eat small mammals, lizards, snakes, fishes, birds, and grasshoppers.

Gavials

The gavial is an odd-looking creature with more teeth than alligators or crocodiles.

There is only one living species of gavial, the Indian gavial, which grows to be 21 feet (6.4 m) long. Although they are very large, gavials eat only fish and are considered to be timid animals. They are found in the river system surrounding the Himalayan Mountains, especially in the Ganges, Brahmaputra, and Indus rivers.

In spite of their great size, gavials are very agile

The black caiman is the largest of the New World crocodilians. It grows to a length of 20 feet (6 m).

and can run quickly on land. At the tip of every gavial's long and very slender snout is a lumpy knob of flesh that contains its nostrils. The gavial uses its long snout to catch fish.

The Indian gavial, or gharial, is an endangered species.

CHAPTER 6
Crocodiles

There are fourteen recognized species of crocodiles. Except for the shape of the snout, crocodiles look very similar to alligators. Alligators have very broad, rounded snouts, while crocodiles have pointed snouts.

A crocodile has no lips and cannot close its mouth tightly. When the crocodile closes its jaws, the fourth long bottom tooth on either side sticks out. It is possible to see where this tooth fits into a groove on the side of the upper jaw. This "special smile" helps us to tell the difference between crocodiles and alligators.

Crocodiles have lungs and breathe through a passage that runs between the back of the throat to the nostrils. Like the alligator, the crocodile has a valve that closes off its air pipe so that water cannot enter its lungs.

*This dwarf crocodile of western Africa has a
"special smile."*

Crocodiles can be found in the areas shaded red.

These animals prefer to live in large bodies of shallow water and are found in sluggish rivers and open swamps and marshes where they feed on fish, turtles, and water birds. The webbed feet of crocodiles allow them to walk on soft, swampy ground.

In very hot, dry weather, crocodiles may go into *estivation*, and in cold weather, they go into hibernation. During these times, the animals' body processes slow down, and they live off stored fat.

Species of Crocodiles

Crocodile	Habitat	Appearance
African dwarf crocodile	West Africa	Up to 6 feet (1.8 m) long; short, somewhat broad snout
Nile crocodile	Tropical and southern Africa; inland rivers of Madagascar	Up to 8 feet (2.4 m) long; moderately sharp snout
Johnston's crocodile (Australian freshwater crocodile)	Australia	Up to 10 feet (3 m) long; head has a triangular outline; narrow, pointed snout
Philippine crocodile	Philippine Islands	Up to 10 feet (3 m) long; broad snout; very rare
Morelet's crocodile	Mexico and Guatemala	10 to 11.5 feet (3 to 3.5 m); bluntly-triangular head; oval snout
Orinoco crocodile	Venezuela	Up to 12 feet (3.7 m) long; slender snout
Cuban crocodile	Cuba	Up to 12 feet (3.7 m) long; bluntly-triangular head; oval snout; extremely fierce
African slender-snouted crocodile	West Africa	10 to 13 feet (3 to 4 m) long; head has a triangular outline; pointed snout
Siamese crocodile	Java, Thailand, and Asia	Up to 13 feet (4 m) long; moderately sharp snout

Crocodile	Habitat	Appearance
False gavial	Freshwater habitats of the Malay Peninsula of Thailand, Malaysia, Sumatra, Borneo, and Java	About 13 feet (4 m) long; slender snout
Marsh crocodile (Mugger)	Inland marshes, rivers, and lakes of India, Sri Lanka, Myanmar, and the Malay Peninsula	Up to 13 feet (4 m) long; short, broad snout; wanders through jungle in times of drought
New Guinea crocodile	Freshwater rivers, lakes, marshes, and swamplands of the Sepik River drainage on the north coast of Papua New Guinea	About 13 feet (4 m) long; tapered snout; brown with black to dark-brown bands or spots on its body and tail*
American crocodile	Florida, southern Mexico, Central America, and northern South America	13 to 18 feet (4 to 5.5 m) long
Indo-Pacific crocodile (Saltwater crocodile)	Coastal marshes and fresh-water lakes and rivers of southern India, Malaysia, the Solomon Islands, and northern Australia	18 to 20 feet (5.5 to 6.1 m) long; prominent ridge in front of each eye; can swim as far as 100 miles (160 km) out to sea; largest and most feared crocodile; known to attack humans

*Although the south coast New Guinea crocodile, referred to as the Papuan, is distinctly different from the New Guinea crocodile, it is not yet recognized as a separate species.

The American Crocodile

The American crocodile is much less common than the American alligator. It is found in the Everglades region of Florida as well as in southern Mexico, Central America, and northern South America. In Ecuador, the American crocodile makes its home in saltwater marshes, large rivers, and lakes.

Like the alligator, the American crocodile is a dark gray-green color. It is more at home in water than on land. Close-set, overlapping, bony plates cover the crocodile's back and neck, and a thick skin covers its underparts. Its eyes and nostrils are on the top of its flat head, allowing the crocodile to see and breathe while remaining hidden in the water.

The nest of the female American crocodile consists of a shallow hole close to the water's edge. After laying her eggs, she covers the nest with sand, mud, and weeds. When she is done, the nest is about as wide as an alligator's, but it is only a few inches high. The temperature inside the crocodile's nest stays just above 100°F (38°C).

Like female alligators, mother crocodiles guard their nests from hungry animals. Mother crocodiles also help their young to break out of the nest upon hearing their grunts. As the mother pushes away the

The American crocodile is far less common than the American alligator.

Like a baby alligator, a baby crocodile uses an egg tooth at the tip of its snout to break through its shell.

Nile crocodiles have been known to catch and eat humans.

material covering the nest, each baby uses its egg-tooth to escape from its shell.

Newly hatched babies are about 8 inches (20 cm) long. They are a light greenish-gray color with black crossbands. By the time they are 6 years old, most American crocodiles are about 6 feet (1.8 m) long. The record length of a crocodile in the United States is 15 feet (4.6 m), while in South America the record is 23 feet (7 m). Crocodiles usually live to be 30 to 40 years old.

The Nile Crocodile

Perhaps the most famous of all the crocodiles is the Nile crocodile. It is reported that some Africans call this crocodile "the animal that kills while it is smiling." Women washing their clothes in the rivers of Africa are sometimes caught and eaten by the Nile crocodile. This crocodile often rests with its mouth open. At one time, scientists thought that the crocodiles were waiting for prey. They now know, however, that they are actually releasing excess body heat.

A very special friend of this animal is the crocodile bird, or ziczac. This bird, which is a relative of the plover, gets this name from its noisy cry. The ziczac picks off and eats little parasites and leeches from the crocodile. The little ziczac will even walk inside a crocodile's open mouth to pick at parasites and walk out again unharmed.

Stones have been found in the stomachs of Nile crocodiles. Some people think that these stones help grind up their food, while others believe the crocodiles deliberately swallow stones to help them keep their balance in the water and to stay submerged for longer periods of time.

The Nile crocodile was worshipped by ancient Egyptians who embalmed these animals and held them sacred. People of each city worshipped a specific crocodile. Today, visitors to New York's Metropolitan Museum of Art can admire a crocodilian mask of wood and see a bronze box made to hold a crocodile mummy.

Like the American crocodile, the Nile crocodile digs a nest near the bank of the river and deposits fifty to sixty eggs. These eggs, which take about 90 days to hatch, are a little larger and less brittle than a hen's eggs. The Nile crocodile must protect its nest from baboons, monitors, and hyenas. These animals are such a threat that the mother crocodile rarely leaves the nest, even to eat.

When the babies hatch, the mother crocodile leads them away from the river into a marshy area with high grass. The babies hide here until they grow large enough to defend themselves.

The female Nile crocodile digs a nest near the bank of a river. She lays fifty to sixty eggs.

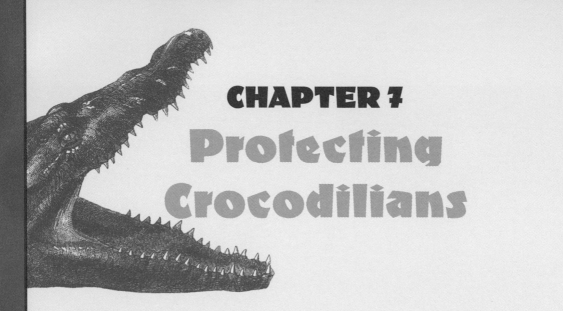

CHAPTER 7

Protecting Crocodilians

Some crocodilian species are in immediate danger of extinction, while others are threatened. In the past, crocodilians everywhere were hunted for their skins (used as leather), for their musk glands (used in perfume), and for their tails (eaten in many parts of the world). Environmental pollution and habitat destruction continue to threaten these reptiles.

The United States Endangered Species Conservation Act of 1969 mandated that a conference be held to draft an international endangered species treaty. In 1973, representatives from eighty-one nations convened at the Convention on International Trade in Endangered Species of Wild Fauna and Flora. The group prohibited the unauthorized importation of wildlife. It also created two lists—one included endangered species and the other included species that might become endangered if trade was not regulated. All crocodilians were placed on one of these two lists.

Although illegal trade in crocodilians still occurs, it has been greatly reduced. Individual countries set quotas that determine how many crocodiles may be killed or collected. Some countries require that self-locking tags be attached to legal skins and that permits for these skins be printed on security paper.

Some crocodilians, including the American alligator, have made remarkable comebacks since they have been placed on endangered species lists. This is fortunate because the crocodilians are among the most interesting of creatures. Their ancient ancestors walked and swam and roared along with the dinosaurs. They were able to survive when the dinosaurs could not, and they are still alive today. They are survivors—living reminders of the Age of Dinosaurs.

Glossary

amphibian—a cold-blooded vertebrate, intermediate in many ways between fishes and reptiles; adults breathe air.

archosaur—a group of reptiles that includes dinosaurs and crocodilians.

clutch—a nest of eggs.

cold-blooded—having a body temperature not internally regulated but approximating that of the environment.

crawl—trail made by an alligator in a swamp or along the bank of a stream.

crocodilian—a group of reptiles that includes alligators and caimans, gavials, and crocodiles.

egg tooth—a hard spike on the tip of the jaw of a baby alligator.

estivation—to pass the summer in a resting state.

evolve—to change and develop physical characteristics over a period of time.

extinction—the process by which all individuals in a species die because they cannot adapt to their environment.

fossil—any trace of an animal or plant from past geological ages that has been preserved in the Earth's crust.

hibernate/hibernation—to pass the winter in a resting state.

nocturnal—active at night.

prey—an animal captured for food.

protosuchian—the earliest ancestor of the crocodilians.

reptile—a class of animals that includes crocodilians as well as turtles, snakes, and lizards.

species—a group of organisms that produce viable offspring when they mate.

torpid—sluggish and lacking motion.

For Further Reading

Bender, Lionel. *Crocodiles and Alligators*. New York: Gloucester Press, 1988.

Brennan, Frank. *Reptiles*. New York: Macmillan, 1992.

Bright, Michael. *Crocodiles and Alligators*. New York: Gloucester Press, 1990.

George, Jean Craighead. *The Moon of the Alligators*. New York: HarperCollins, 1991.

Ross, C. A., ed. *Crocodiles and Alligators*. New York: Facts on File, 1989.

Taylor, Dave. *The Alligator and the Everglades*. Toronto: Crabtree Publishing Co., 1990.

Tibbitts, Alison, and Alan Roocroft. *Crocodiles*. Mankato, MN: Capstone Press, 1992.

Index

About The Author

Phyllis J. Perry has worked as an elementary school teacher and principal and has written two dozen books for teachers and young people. Her most recent books for Franklin Watts are *Sea Star and Dragons* and *Ballooning*. She received her doctorate in Curriculum and Instruction from the University of Colorado, where she supervises student teachers. Dr. Perry lives with her husband, David, in Boulder, Colorado.